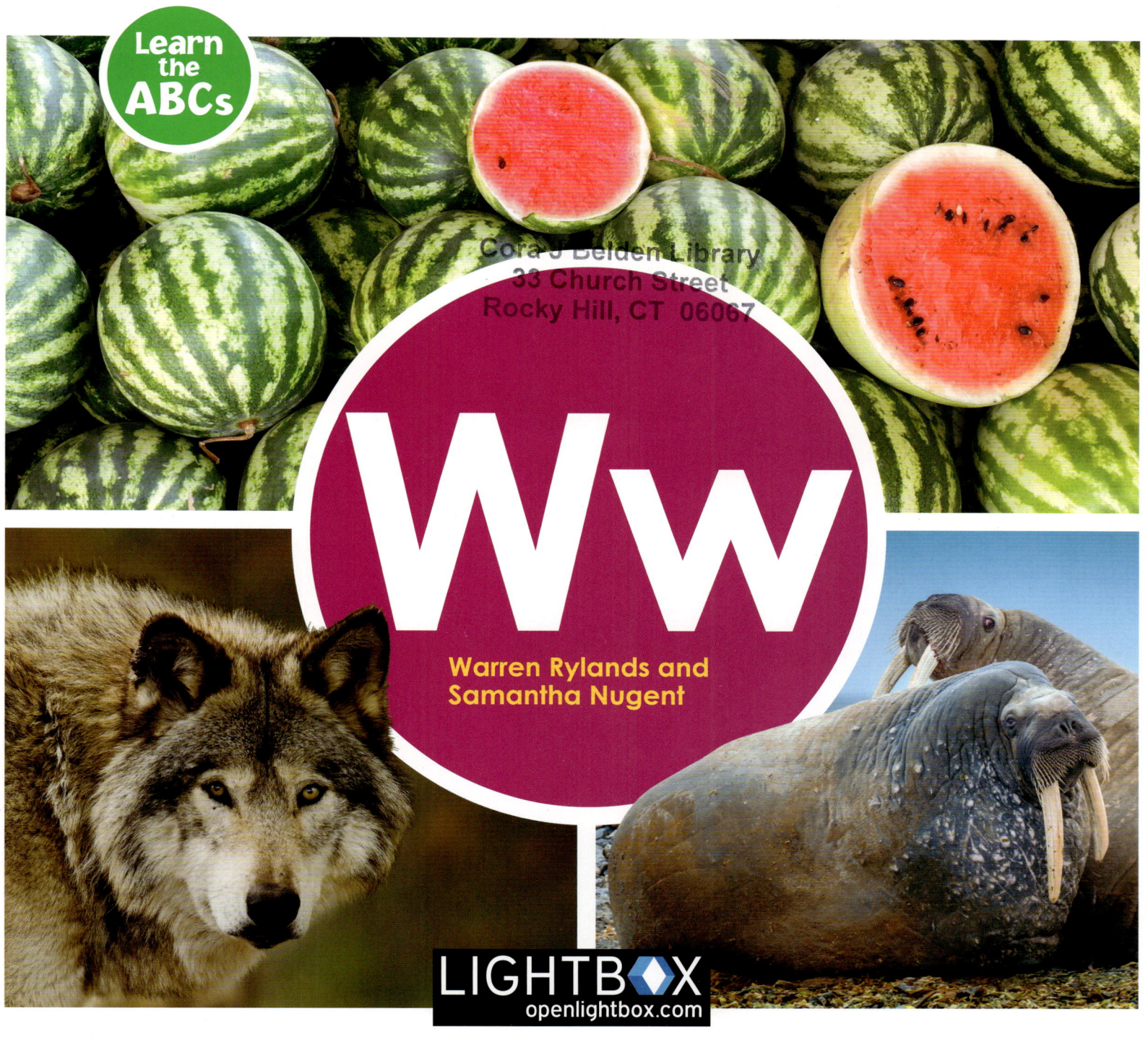

Learn the ABCs

Ww

Warren Rylands and
Samantha Nugent

LIGHTBOX
openlightbox.com

LIGHTBOX

Go to
www.openlightbox.com
and enter this book's
unique code.

ACCESS CODE

L B X Z 5 9 9 8

Lightbox is an all-inclusive digital solution for the teaching and learning of curriculum topics in an original, groundbreaking way. Lightbox is based on National Curriculum Standards.

OPTIMIZED FOR
✓ **TABLETS**
✓ **WHITEBOARDS**
✓ **COMPUTERS**
✓ **AND MUCH MORE!**

STANDARD FEATURES OF LIGHTBOX

🔊 **AUDIO** High-quality narration using text-to-speech system

▶ **VIDEOS** Embedded high-definition video clips

✒ **ACTIVITIES** Printable PDFs that can be emailed and graded

🌐 **WEBLINKS** Curated links to external, child-safe resources

📖 **SLIDESHOWS** Pictorial overviews of key concepts

✂ **INTERACTIVE MAPS** Interactive maps and aerial satellite imagery

QUIZ **QUIZZES** Ten multiple choice questions that are automatically graded and emailed for teacher assessment

🔑 **KEY WORDS** Matching key concepts to their definitions

VIDEOS

WEBLINKS
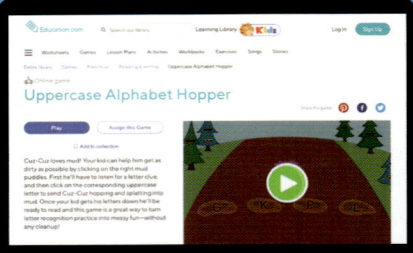

SLIDESHOWS

QUIZZES

This title is part of our Lightbox digital subscription

1-Year K–5 Subscription
ISBN 978-1-5105-5712-3

Access hundreds of Lightbox titles with our digital subscription.
Sign up for a **FREE** subscription trial at **www.openlightbox.com/trial**

Learn the ABCs

Ww

CONTENTS

Let's discover the letter

This is an uppercase W

This is how you write it

This is a lowercase w

This is how you write it

The letter **W** can start many words.

walrus

wolf

watermelon

wagon

worm

The letter **W** can be inside a word.

owl

two

tower

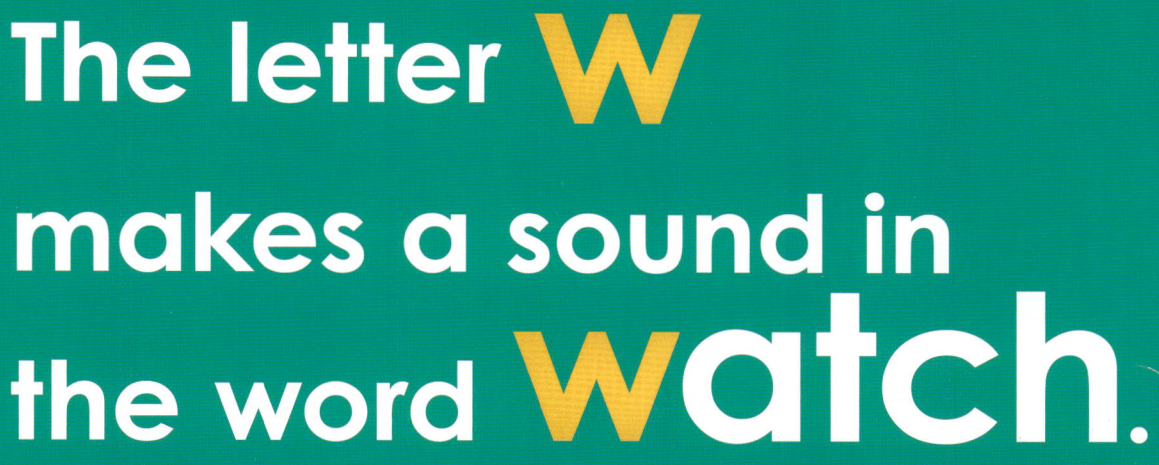

The letter **W** makes a sound in the word **watch**.

The letter **W** does not make a sound in the word **sword**.

The letter **W** makes a sound in most words.

water

we

between

away

work

17

Sometimes, the letter **W** does not make a sound.

write

saw

know

answer

who

Having Fun with W

Warren grows yellow watermelons. He waters them on Wednesday.

One week, Warren went away.

Wilma said she would watch the watermelons.

When Warren came home, the watermelons were white!

Wilma had watered them with her bath water.

The alphabet has **26** letters.

W is the twenty-third letter in the alphabet.

Aa Bb Cc Dd

Ee Ff Gg Hh Ii Jj

Kk Ll Mm Nn Oo

Pp Qq Rr Ss Tt Uu

Vv **Ww** Xx Yy Zz

KEY WORDS

Research has shown that as much as 65 percent of all written material published in English is made up of 300 words. These 300 words cannot be taught using pictures or learned by sounding them out. They must be recognized by sight. This book contains 60 common sight words to help young readers improve their reading fluency and comprehension. This book also teaches young readers several important content words, such as proper nouns. These words are paired with pictures to aid in learning and improve understanding.

Page	Sight Words First Appearance
4	let, letter, the
5	a, an, how, is, it, this, write, you
6	can, many, start, words
8	be, two
10	at, end, of
12	big, books, has, likes, names, with
14	make, or, sound, watch
15	does, in, not
16	most, water
17	away, between, we, work
18	sometimes
19	answer, know, saw, who
20	grows, he, on, one, said, she, them, went, would
21	came, had, her, home, were, when, white

Page	Content Words First Appearance
4	Ww
6	walrus
7	wagon, watermelon, wolf, worm
8	owl, tower
9	twins, yawn
10	elbow, snow
11	cow, window, yellow
12	smile, Warren, Wilma
13	bread, mask, Wendy, Whitney, Will
14	sword
20	fun, Wednesday, week
21	bath
22	alphabet

Published by Smartbook Media Inc.
276 5th Avenue, Suite 704 #917
New York, NY 10001
Website: www.openlightbox.com

Library of Congress Cataloging-in-Publication Data

Names: Rylands, Warren, author. | Nugent, Samantha, author. | Nugent, Samantha, author.
Title: Ww / Warren Rylands and Samantha Nugent.
Description: New York, NY : Smartbook Media Inc., [2022] | Series: Learn the ABCs | Audience: Grades K-1.
Identifiers: LCCN 2020054114 (print) | LCCN 2020054115 (ebook) | ISBN 9781510558014 (library binding) | ISBN 9781510558038 (ebook other)

Subjects: LCSH: English language--Consonants--Juvenile literature.
Classification: LCC PE1165 .R9545 2022 (print) | LCC PE1165 (ebook) | DDC 428/.13--dc23
LC record available at https://lccn.loc.gov/2020054114
LC ebook record available at https://lccn.loc.gov/2020054115

Printed in Guangzhou, China
1 2 3 4 5 6 7 8 9 0   25 24 23 22 21

022021
110820

Art Director: Terry Paulhus   **Project Coordinator:** Sara Cucini

Every reasonable effort has been made to trace ownership and to obtain permission to reprint copyright material. The publisher would be pleased to have any errors or omissions brought to its attention so that they may be corrected in subsequent printings.

The publisher acknowledges Getty Images as the primary image supplier for this title.